colorful crochet
afghans and pillows

Kristel Salgarollo

STACKPOLE
BOOKS

Contents

THE PROJECTS

Author's Note

To Our Mien (Grandmother)

My grandmother was an independent and creative woman, passionate about fiber crafts. Continually living hand-to-mouth, she used and reused everything she could, always succeeding in creating something from nothing. She had a sense for the possibilities of repurposing long before "upcycling" became a trend—and a sense of style that was . . . let's say "colorful"!

I still have a photo of her wearing one of her crocheted dresses, in which she had used more than a hundred different colors of yarn. Sitting on her couch in the middle of her collection of homemade pillows—themselves multicolored—she blended right into her surroundings so you could hardly tell where Mien ended and the pillows began!

Her house looked like Pippi Longstocking's. I remember in particular rugs crocheted from old nylon stockings, surprisingly durable, but which certainly looked zany to the eyes of us kids. Today, I'm so sorry I didn't keep anything from this extravagant universe, which would be all the rage now with the popularity of vintage and handmade items!

Like the adage says, "the apple doesn't fall far from the tree," and of Mien's three granddaughters (my sisters and I), two of us shared the same love of fiber arts, even making our living from them (incidentally, my youngest sister, Inez, named her boutique after our Mien), and the third one paints. The one great-granddaughter who also inherited the same uncontrolled love of fiber arts is probably the one who will take up the torch after her aunts.

In my case, the fascination started very early. I was just six years old when I caught a glimpse of the possibilities offered by crochet thanks to a classmate and her extraordinary lilac and mint green pullover, which I couldn't take my eyes off. Still, I was fourteen before I started crocheting all kinds of tunics for myself and my friends. I worked without a pattern, following my inspiration, a bit as Mien had done. But who would be surprised at that, at the beginning of the 1970s, at the height of "flower power"?

In my last year of high school, I made a whole granny-square afghan during math class—contrary to what I'd declared just a little while earlier, school finally gave me the opportunity to advance in my art. Sitting in the last row, I slyly crocheted under my desk! Needless to say, my end-of-the-year exams were not brilliant, leading my teacher to say that I would never go far in life. He would surely be happy to learn that with the little bit of knowledge of logarithms and integrals that he managed to impart to me despite myself, I succeeded in making something of myself.

Many of you know me for my work in quilting, which I discovered later on. You now know everything (or almost everything) about how I took up crochet—and I never put it down. I always have a project on my hook, and I bring it along with me in the car, on the train, or in the waiting rooms that today have replaced math class for me! The portability of crochet is one of the great pleasures and advantages of the craft.

When, six years ago, I decided to expand my store so I could offer wool and cotton yarn in addition to quilting fabrics, I never dreamed that crochet and knitting would experience such a resurgence in popularity that they would break out of the little circle they had occupied and steal the hearts of so many young mothers and hip young women.

Author's Note

I'm not a grandmother yet, and I'm not a young mother anymore. My three daughters have left home, but each has one of my crocheted afghans to curl up in. Now I'm eager to start spoiling grandkids. There are so many beautiful things to make for little ones!

I plan to keep crocheting (as well as quilting and everything else) for a long time still; I'm not running out of ideas, and I already have enough to keep me busy for the next hundred years!

I'm thrilled to be able to share this bit of my own story with you, and I hope you enjoy creating the beautiful projects in this book.

Finally, I would like to extend a huge thank you to my sister Inez, who was kind enough to crochet my Grandmother's Flower Garden design into a real afghan, patiently crocheting the innumerable little hexagons and weaving in all those little ends.

Kristel Salgarollo

Making a Pillow Cover

Note: The sizes are given without seam allowances. Add a seam allowance of ⅜ in. (1 cm) on every edge except for the ones with hems.

For the front, cut a rectangle (or a square) of fabric the same width (*a*) and height (*b*) as the pillow.

For the back, cut one rectangle measuring *a* by (*b*/2) + ⅝ in. (1.5 cm) (for the hem). Cut a second rectangle measuring *a* by (*b*/2) + 1¾ in. (4.5 cm)—⅝ in. (1.5 cm) for the hem and a little more than 1 in. (2.5 cm) for the overlap between the two pieces.

Tip: The bigger the piece, the more important the overlap between the two back pieces is. I recommend you adapt the measurements given here to give more overlap for larger projects.

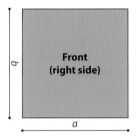
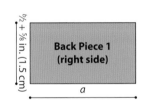

Make a double hem along the top edge of one of the back pieces (first fold back ¼ in. [6 mm], then fold back another ⅜ in. [1 cm]) and sew the hem. Do the same on the other back piece.

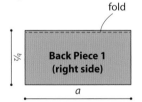
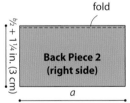

Place the front and the back pieces together (with the back pieces overlapping by about 1 in. [2.5 cm] in the middle), with right sides together, and sew all the way around the edge. Turn the cover right side out.

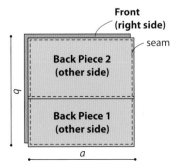

Sew the crocheted piece on the front with blind stitch.

MAKING THE PROJECTS

For the projects made out of smaller motifs, each motif only requires a small amount of yarn. You can change the yarn colors and the sizes of the projects as you please for different uses.

1. The amounts of yarn required and the finished measurements given in each pattern are approximate. Depending on how tightly or loosely you crochet, these may change for your projects.

2. Once you've made one motif, compare its size to the size given in the gauge information. If they're the same size, your project will match the measurements given. If your motif is larger, try working with a smaller hook; if it's smaller, try a larger hook.

3. Look at the additional skills on page 9 before beginning.

Basic Stitches and Symbols

Slip Knot

Step 1: Position the crochet hook behind the yarn and turn the hook as indicated by the arrow to wrap the yarn around the hook.

Step 2: Hold the loop formed with your thumb and fingers. Then wrap the yarn around the hook as shown in the diagram (we will call this motion "yarning over" from now on).

Step 3: Draw the yarn through the loop.

Step 4: Pull down on the end of the yarn to close the knot around the base of the loop just formed.

Step 5: The slip knot—the beginning loop—is complete.

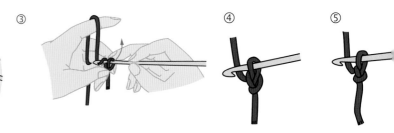

⬯ Chain Stitch (ch)

Step 1: Yarn over, moving the hook in the direction shown in the diagram.

Step 2: Draw the yarn through the loop already on the hook to form the first chain.

Step 3: Yarn over and pull through the new loop to form the second chain.

Step 4: Repeat as many times as indicated in the pattern.

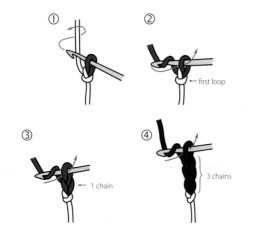

⬮ Slip Stitch (sl st)

Step 1: Insert the hook into the next stitch in the direction shown by the arrow in the diagram. (In this case, we are working into the first stitch of a row.)

Step 2: Yarn over, then draw the yarn back through the stitch and loop at the same time, following the arrow. One slip stitch is complete.

Step 3: To make another slip stitch, insert the hook into the next stitch (shown by the arrow) and repeat step 2.

Step 4: Continue as many times as indicated in the pattern. This stitch tends to be rather tight; to avoid this, work loosely by pulling each loop a little longer than you normally would.

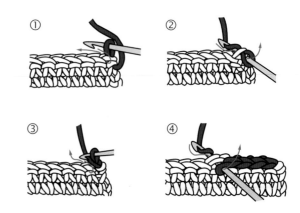

⊠ Single Crochet (sc)

Step 1: If working at the beginning of a row, ch 1 (turning chain) before inserting the hook in the next stitch. (In the diagram, we are working into a foundation chain.)

Step 2: Yarn over and draw the yarn through the stitch.

Step 3: Yarn over again and draw the yarn through both loops.

Step 4: The first single crochet is complete. Insert the hook into the next stitch and repeat steps 2 and 3 to continue working.

Step 5: 3 single crochets completed.

⊤ Half Double Crochet (hdc)

Step 1: At the beginning of a row, start with 2 turning chains, which will count as the first half double crochet. Yarn over, then insert the hook in the 4th chain from the hook.

Step 2: Yarn over and draw the yarn through the stitch. Yarn over again and draw the yarn through all the loops on the hook.

Step 3: The first half double crochet is complete. Yarn over and insert the hook into the next stitch, then repeat step 2 to continue working.

Step 4: 4 half double crochets completed (2 turning chains which count as the first half double crochet, and 3 regular half double crochets).

⊤ Double Crochet (dc)

Step 1: Start with 3 turning chains for the first double crochet. Yarn over, then insert the hook in the 5th chain from the hook, as indicated by the arrow in the diagram.

Step 2: Yarn over and draw the yarn through the stitch.

Step 3: Yarn over and draw the yarn through the first two loops on the hook.

Step 4: Yarn over and draw the yarn through the two remaining loops on the hook.

Step 5: The first double crochet is complete. Yarn over and insert the hook into the next stitch, then repeat steps 2 to 4 to continue working. Diagram 5 shows 4 completed double crochets (3 turning chains which count as the first double crochet, and 3 regular double crochets)

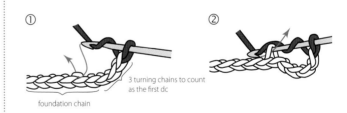

Basic Stitches and Symbols

Treble Crochet (tr)

Step 1: If working at the beginning of a row, start with 4 turning chains for the first treble crochet. Yarn over twice, then insert the hook in the 6th chain from the hook, as indicated by the arrow in the diagram.

Step 2: Yarn over and draw the yarn through the stitch. Yarn over again and draw the yarn through the first two loops on the hook.

Step 3: Yarn over and draw the yarn through the next two loops on the hook.

Step 4: Yarn over and draw the yarn through the two remaining loops on the hook. The first treble crochet is complete.

Step 5: Yarn over and insert the hook into the next stitch, then repeat steps 2 to 4 to continue working.

Step 6: 4 treble crochets completed (4 turning chains which count as the first treble crochet, and 3 regular treble crochets).

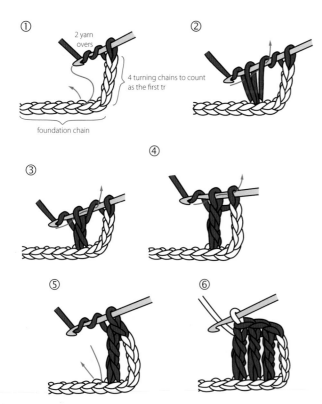

Turning Chains

At the beginning of each row of crochet, the first stitch is replaced by an equivalent number of chains (except for with single crochet). The diagrams below show the number of chains to work to substitute for each stitch.

Single	Half Double	Double	Treble
5 stitches	5 stitches	5 stitches	5 stitches
1 ch	2 chs	3 chs	4 chs

Working in the Round

There are two techniques for starting a piece that will be worked in the round.

Magic Loop

① ② ③

Step 1: Wrap the yarn loosely around your index finger to form a double loop, then insert the hook through this loop. Yarn over and pull the yarn up through the loop.

Step 2: Yarn over and pull the yarn through the loop already on the hook.

Step 3: The magic ring is ready to work into. Insert your hook through the middle of the ring when you would normally be inserting it into a stitch. When you have worked the number of stitches indicated in the pattern, pull on the end of the yarn to tighten the loop.

Ring of Chains

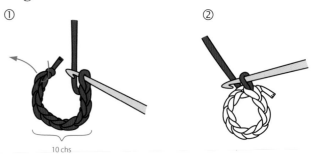

10 chs

Step 1: Work the number of chains indicated (here, 10), then insert the hook through the first chain.

Step 2: Work a slip stitch to join the chain into a ring. To work into the ring of chains, insert your hook through the middle of the ring (not into the chains themselves) when you would normally be inserting it into a stitch.

Additional Skills

CHANGING YARN

There are two ways to change to a new color or ball of yarn. Use whichever one gives you the look you prefer.

Basic Method

①

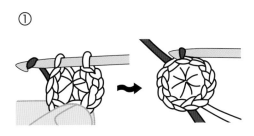

Work up to the final yarn over of the last round or row in the old color. Yarn over with the new color and finish the last stitch (here, a slip stitch joining the end of the round to the beginning) with the new color. Continue in the new color to work the second round.

Variation

②

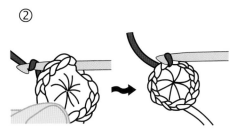

Finish the entire round in the old color and fasten the work off by cutting the yarn, pulling the end through the loop, and pulling tight. Make a slip knot with the new yarn and work a slip stitch in the stitch where you want to start working in the new color to join it. This method allows you to change where the rounds begin.

ASSEMBLING PIECES WITH OVERCAST STITCH

This technique is used to attach geometric motifs with long sides, such as squares or hexagons, together.

① ② ③

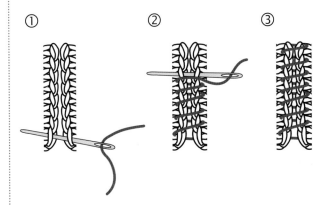

Step 1: Place the motifs side by side with right sides up. Using a yarn needle threaded with yarn, insert the needle through corresponding stitches on the last round or row of both pieces.

Step 2: Bring the needle back around and insert it through the next pair of stitches in the same direction.

Step 3: Continue in this pattern all the way up the seam.

Afghans

Hourglasses and Windmills

Composed of triangles assembled into squares, this classic quilt pattern, worked in bold colors for all four seasons, fits in perfectly with today's styles.

Materials

- 3.5 oz./100 g #1 super fine weight wool yarn in each of the following colors: maroon, brown, ecru, khaki, lime green, dark khaki, orange, red, mustard yellow, beige, and dark brown
- US E-4 (3.5 mm) crochet hook (or size needed to obtain gauge)

Gauge

1 square motif = 4¼ by 4¼ in. (11 by 11 cm)

Measurements

See diagram below.

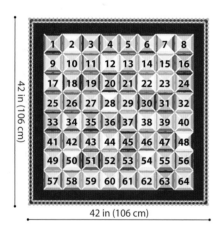

42 in (106 cm)

42 in (106 cm)

Instructions

1. Start with a magic loop. Work triangle **a** (see the gray part of the opposite diagram).

2. Beginning with triangle **b**, join the last row of each triangle to the previous motif(s) with slip stitches, as shown in the diagram. Work triangles **c** and **d** to complete the square motif.

3. For the colors shown here, see the table on page 14.

4. Crochet the square motifs in the order shown in the Measurements diagram.

Assembling the Square Motifs

Work the sl st in the chain space of the neighboring motif.

Start the next motif in the starting loop of the previous motif.

❖ For how to change colors, see page 9.

◀ cut the yarn   ◁ join the yarn

Square Motif

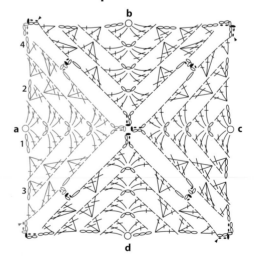

Hourglasses and Windmills

5. For the border, work 7 rounds of double crochet in dark brown around the entire edge of the blanket, then 3 rows of shell pattern (the first in beige, the second in maroon, and the last in mustard yellow), as shown in the diagram opposite.

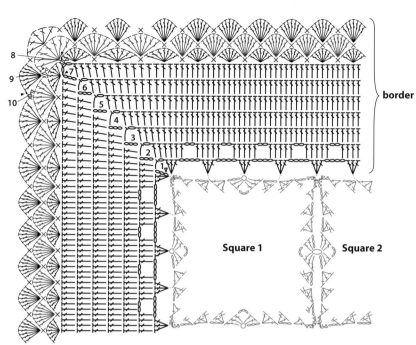

Colors Shown

Square Number	Motifs A and C	Motifs B and D
1 and 45	brown	maroon
2	khaki	ecru
3	maroon	lime green
4 and 47	orange	dark khaki
5	khaki	red
6 and 35	mustard yellow	maroon
7 and 50	dark khaki	ecru
8	beige	khaki
9	lime green	red
10 and 49	mustard yellow	orange
11 and 26	red	brown
12	ecru	mustard yellow
13, 39 and 55	lime green	brown
14	beige	orange
15 and 42	red	lime green
16	brown	dark khaki
17 and 34	ecru	dark khaki
18	maroon	beige
19	dark khaki	khaki
20	beige	maroon
21 and 31	red	dark khaki
22	ecru	khaki
23 and 62	mustard yellow	beige
24 and 33	orange	maroon
25	mustard yellow	khaki

Square Number	Motifs A and C	Motifs B and D
27	lime green	orange
28	brown	ecru
29 and 64	orange	mustard yellow
30	maroon	brown
32	khaki	lime green
36	red	khaki
37	dark khaki	lime green
38	ecru	beige
40 and 49	orange	mustard yellow
41	khaki	brown
43	beige	brown
44 and 60	ecru	orange
46	mustard yellow	red
48	maroon	ecru
51	maroon	red
52	red	mustard yellow
53	khaki	dark khaki
54	orange	ecru
56	dark khaki	beige
57	red	beige
58	mustard yellow	brown
59	beige	lime green
61	brown	lime green
63	khaki	maroon

Flowers and Braids

A polka-dotted backing folded over to form a border, a subtly textured central panel, and appliqué flowers: Everything here celebrates the rediscovered styles of days gone by.

Materials

- 14 oz./400 g #1 super fine weight ecru wool yarn
- Small amounts of #1 super fine weight cotton yarn in the following colors: red, maroon, magenta, fuchsia, coral, yellow, orange, dark orange, light green, medium green, and dark green
- Red fabric with white polka dots, 43 by 52 in. (108 by 133 cm)
- 35 by 45 in. (89 by 114 cm) batting
- Red embroidery floss
- Green cotton quilting thread
- US E-4 (3.5 mm) crochet hook (or size needed to obtain gauge)

Gauge

1 pattern repeat x 7 rows = 2¾ by 2¾ in. (7 by 7 cm)

Measurements

See diagram below.

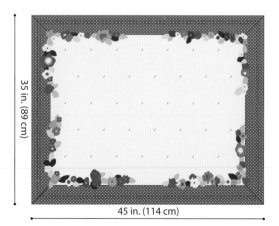

35 in. (89 cm)

45 in. (114 cm)

Flowers and Braids

Instructions

1. For the main piece, start with a foundation chain of 208 chains in ecru. Work 74 rows in the pattern (as shown at right). You should obtain a rectangle 27 by 37 in. (69 by 95 cm).

2. Lay out the main piece with the wrong side up, then center the batting on top of it and sew the two together. Place these two pieces (with right side up) in the center of the backing fabric (wrong side up). Fold the edges of the fabric over onto the main piece as shown in the diagrams below so that the whole thing measures 35 by 45 in. (89 by 114 cm).

Stitch Pattern

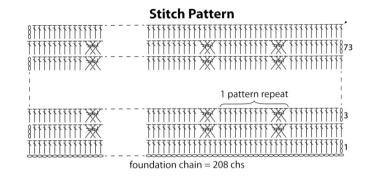

foundation chain = 208 chs

 Cable: skip 2 sts, tr in each of the next 2 sts; working behind the 2 sts just made, tr in the first skipped st and then in the second skipped st.

Making the Folded Border

Place the main piece and batting (right side up) in the center of the backing fabric (wrong side up) and baste. Fold over the fabric ¼ in. (0.5 cm) along each edge.

Fold in the corners to the edges of the main piece. Fold the excess backing fabric on each side in along the dotted lines, to produce borders. Repeat on the top and bottom edges.

Blind stitch the borders (including the corners). Remove the basting stitches.

3. Use the embroidery thread to tie knots 4 in. (10 cm) apart across the main piece, going through all 3 layers of the afghan. With the green quilting thread, work 2 rows of quilting stitch around the edge (see the photo on page 19).

4. Crochet 63 leaves and 65 flowers following the patterns below (mixing up the colors and styles as suits your fancy). **Note:** Leave a long tail on each flower to use for attaching it to the afghan.

5. Arrange the flowers and leaves around the edge of the border, like a garland (see the photo on page 19 for ideas) and sew them down, sewing the flowers in their centers and the leaves along their veins with hidden stitches so that the stitching is not visible on the back of the blanket.

Author's note: For the flowers, I drew inspiration from the book 100 Flowers to Knit and Crochet *by Lesley Stanfield.*

Flower 1

Flower 2

Flower 3

Flower 4

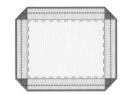

Flower 5

Flower 6

Leaf 1

foundation chain = 7 chs

Leaf 2

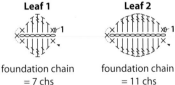

foundation chain = 11 chs

◄ cut the yarn

4-treble popcorn: Work 4 tr in the next stitch; stretch out the working loop and remove it from the hook; insert the hook through the first tr from front to back, then pick up the dropped loop and pull it through the stitch, pulling on the thread to tighten it.

Double crochet 2 together (dc2tog): Work 2 incomplete dc in the next stitch (leaving the last loop on the hook); yarn over and draw through all 3 remaining loops at once.

Treble crochet 2 together (tr2tog): Work 2 incomplete tr in the next stitch (leaving the last loop on the hook; yarn over and draw through all 3 remaining loops at once.

Double crochet 3 together (dc3tog): Work 3 incomplete dc in the next stitch (leaving the last loop on the hook); yarn over and draw through all 4 remaining loops at once.

Multicolored Waves

Row after row, unfurl these waves in pastels and jewel tones and become an expert at this zigzag stitch pattern!

Materials

- 4.5 oz./125 g #2 fine weight wool yarn in the following colors: light blue, beige, slate gray, blue gray, light khaki, ivory, mauve, maroon, lime green, navy blue, and medium blue
- 1.75 oz./50 g #2 fine weight wool yarn in magenta
- US E-4 (3.5 mm) crochet hook (or size needed to obtain gauge)

Gauge

1 pattern repeat x 7 rows = 4 by 4 in. (10 by 10 cm)

Measurements

See diagram below.

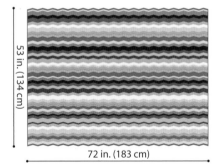

53 in. (134 cm)

72 in. (183 cm)

Multicolored Waves

Instructions

1. Start with a foundation chain of 604 chs and work 102 rows in the wave pattern (see diagram).

2. For the color changes, see the table below.

3. For the border, work 1 round of double crochet in magenta all the way around the edge, as shown in the diagram.

❖ For how to change colors, see page 9. Work directly in the stitch indicated (without working a sl st).

◀ cut the yarn

◁ join the yarn

Wave Pattern

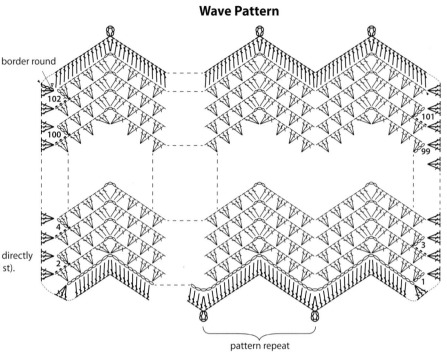

Color Pattern

Rows	Color
1–2 25–26 50 74–75 102	light blue
3–4 29 54–55 79–80	beige
5–6 27–28 51–53 76–78	slate gray
7–8 30–31 56–57 81–82	blue gray
9–11 32–33 58 83–85	light khaki
12–13 34–36 59–60 86–87	ivory

Rows	Color
14–15 37–38 61–63 88–89	mauve
16 39–41 64 90–92	maroon
17–19 42–43 65–66 93–94	lime green
20–21 44–45 67–68 95–96	magenta
22 46–47 69–71 97–98	navy blue
23–24 48–49 72–73 99–101	medium blue

Rainbow Zigzags

Have double the fun by combining knitting and crochet to create this sweet rainbow piece, which makes a great bedside rug.

Materials

- 9 oz./250 g #4 medium weight gray wool yarn
- 1 oz./25 g #4 medium weight wool yarn in the following colors: lime green, light green, light beige, beige, yellow, orange, dark orange, rose, red, and dark red
- US H-8 (5.0 mm) crochet hook (or size needed to obtain gauge)
- US 8 (5.0 mm) 24 in. circular knitting needle

Gauge

1 pattern repeat x 9 rows in crochet = 4¾ by 4 in. (12 by 10 cm)
16 sts x 18 rows in stockinette stitch = 4 by 4 in. (10 by 10 cm)

Measurements

See diagram below.

25 in. (64 cm)

68 in. (173 cm)

Instructions

1. With the crochet hook and the dark red yarn, work a foundation chain of 106 chs. Work 31 rows of zigzag stitch (see diagram below).

Zigzag Stitch

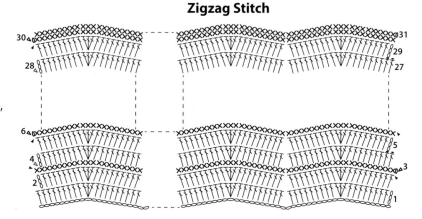

❖ For how to change colors, see page 9.

◀ cut the yarn　　　△ join the yarn

2. For the color changes, see the table below.

Color Pattern

Rows	Color
1–2	dark red
3, 6, 9, 12, 15, 18, 21, 24, 27, 30, 31	gray
4–5	red
7–8	rose
10–11	dark orange
13–14	orange
16–17	yellow
19–20	beige
22–23	light beige
25–26	light green
28–29	lime green

Rainbow Zigzags

3. With the knitting needles and gray, pick up 105 sts along the top of the crocheted section and work in stockinette stitch (Row 1: Knit every stitch; Row 2: Purl every stitch. Repeat these 2 rows for pattern.) for 36 in. (92 cm). Bind off all stitches.

4. Work 31 rows of the zigzag pattern as in step 1, following the same color order, alternating a gray row of sc every 3 rows.

5. Use overcast stitch (see page 9) to join the zigzag portion to the gray knitted section.

Grandmother's Flower Garden

Grandmother's Flower Garden

A translation of a beloved traditional quilt pattern, this large afghan, entirely made up of hexagons, is full of tender memories.

Materials

- 28 oz./800 g #1 super fine cotton yarn in black
- 3.5 oz./100 g #1 super fine cotton yarn in the following colors: light pink, magenta, orange, dark red, fuchsia, peach, medium green, coral, red, dark orange, dark khaki, apple green, and medium pink
- US E-4 (3.5 mm) crochet hook (or size needed to obtain gauge)

Gauge

1 hexagon motif = 1¾ by 2¼ in. (4.5 by 5.5 cm)

Measurements

See diagram below.

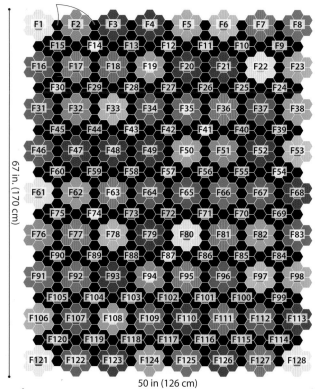

background motifs (B)

67 in. (170 cm)

50 in (126 cm)

Instructions

1. Start each motif with a magic loop. Each flower is formed of 7 hexagonal motifs (6 motifs of one color for the petals and central motif in a different color).

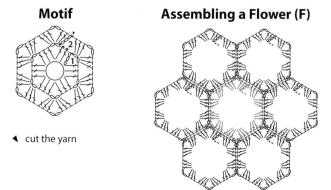

Motif

◄ cut the yarn

Assembling a Flower (F)

2. For the colors, **see the chart below**.

Colors Shown

Background	128 black motifs
F1	6 light pink motifs, 1 apple green motif
F2	6 apple green motifs, 1 dark red motif
F3	6 dark red motifs, 1 medium green motif
F4	6 fuchsia motifs, 1 orange motif
F5, F98, F106	6 orange motifs, 1 magenta motif
F6	6 peach motifs, 1 medium green motif
F7	6 dark orange motifs, 1 medium pink motif
F8, F91	6 medium green motifs, 1 magenta motif
F9, F29, F40, F59	6 black motifs, 1 dark red motif
F10, F27, F39, F56, F69, F85, F101, F117	6 black motifs, 1 dark orange motif
F11, F24, F60	6 black motifs, 1 medium pink motif
F12, F75, F89, F103, F120	6 black motifs, 1 coral motif
F13, F73, F102	6 black motifs, 1 fuchsia motif
F14, F41, F54, F74, F87	6 black motifs, 1 light pink motif
F15, F44, F72, F100	6 black motifs, 1 dark khaki motif
F16	6 magenta motifs, 1 dark red motif

continued on page 30

Grandmother's Flower Garden

Colors Shown

F17	6 medium pink motifs, 1 dark khaki motif
F18	6 dark orange motifs, 1 red motif
F19, F108	6 coral motifs, 1 light pink motif
F20, F79	6 dark red motifs, 1 magenta motif
F21	6 dark khaki motifs, 1 apple green motif
F22	6 light pink motifs, 1 peach motif
F23	6 orange motifs, 1 apple green motif
F25, F86, F118	6 black motifs, 1 medium green motif
F26, F45, F55, F84, F115	6 black motifs, 1 red motif
F28, F104	6 black motifs, 1 orange motif
F30, F43, F57	6 black motifs, 1 peach motif
F31, F112	6 magenta motifs, 1 fuchsia motif
F32	6 apple green motifs, 1 fuchsia motif
F33, F53	6 peach motifs, 1 magenta motif
F34	6 magenta motifs, 1 medium green motif
F35	6 medium green motifs, 1 light pink motif
F36, F81	6 medium pink motifs, 1 dark orange motif
F37	6 red motifs, 1 dark red motif
F38	6 coral motifs, 1 medium pink motif
F42	6 black motifs, 1 apple green motif
F46	6 red motifs, 1 magenta motif
F47	6 dark khaki motifs, 1 medium pink motif
F48	6 fuchsia motifs, 1 apple green motif
F49	6 dark red motifs, 1 dark orange motif
F50	6 orange motifs, 1 light pink motif
F51	6 apple green motifs, 1 dark orange motif
F52	6 fuchsia motifs, 1 medium pink motif
F58, F70, F88, F99, F105, F116, F119	6 black motifs, 1 magenta motif
F61	6 light pink motifs, 1 dark orange motif
F62	6 coral motifs, 1 dark khaki motif
F63	6 medium pink motifs, 1 light pink motif
F64, F67	6 magenta motifs, 1 dark orange motif
F65	6 red motifs, 1 peach motif

F66	6 medium green motifs, 1 dark red motif
F68	6 dark khaki motifs, 1 orange motif
F71, F90, F114	6 black motifs, 1 apple green motif
F76	6 apple green motifs, 1 red motif
F77	6 medium pink motifs, 1 fuchsia motif
F78	6 peach motifs, 1 orange motif
F80	6 light pink motifs, 1 red motif
F82	6 coral motifs, 1 fuchsia motif
F83	6 magenta motifs, 1 light pink motif
F92	6 dark orange motifs, 1 fuchsia motif
F93	6 fuchsia motifs, 1 dark khaki motif
F94	6 apple green motifs, 1 light pink motif
F95	6 medium pink motifs, 1 coral motif
F96	6 red motifs, 1 medium green motif
F97	6 peach motifs, 1 apple green motif
F107	6 red motifs, 1 fuchsia motif
F109	6 magenta motifs, 1 apple green motif
F110	6 dark red motifs, 1 coral motif
F111	6 dark orange motifs, 1 apple green motif
F113	6 dark khaki motifs, 1 orange motif
F121	6 light pink motifs, 1 dark khaki motif
F122	6 magenta motifs, 1 orange motif
F123	6 dark red motifs, 1 peach motif
F124	6 coral motifs, 1 red motif
F125	6 medium green motifs, 1 peach motif
F126	6 fuchsia motifs, 1 peach motif
F127	6 dark orange motifs, 1 dark red motif
F128	6 light pink motifs, 1 magenta motif

3. Assemble the flowers with overcast stitch (see page 9). Then assemble the flowers and the extra background motifs (B) that go in between them with overcast stitch.

Assembling the Flowers and Background Motifs

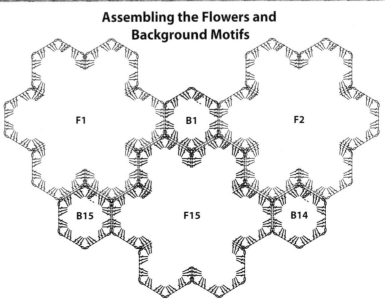

F1   B1   F2

B15   F15   B14

Log Cabins with Clear Skies

Play with contrasts by placing warm and cool shades together, and trade the red centers usually used in this quilt pattern for a sky blue.

Materials

- 3.5 oz./100 g #3 light weight wool yarn (shown in Felted Tweed DK by Rowan) in the following colors: sky blue (**SB**), ocean blue (**OB**), navy blue (**NB**), beige (**BE**), dark orange (**DO**), dark green (**DG**), lime green (**LG**), gold (**G**), slate gray (**SG**), purple (**PU**), brown (**BR**), peach (**PE**), mauve (**MA**), medium blue (**MB**), blue gray (**BG**), and ecru (**E**)
- 9 oz./250 g #3 light weight wool yarn (shown in Felted Tweed DK by Rowan) in dark red (**DR**)
- US E-4 (3.5 mm) crochet hook (or size needed to obtain gauge)

Gauge

1 motif = 9 by 9 in. (22 by 22 cm)

Measurements

See diagram below.

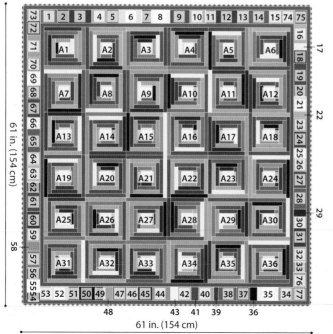

Log Cabins with Clear Skies

Instructions

1. Starting with a magic loop, crochet 36 **square** motifs as shown in the diagram at right. For the colors to use, see the next section.

Colors Shown

For all the square motifs, work **Rounds 1–3** in sky blue, then work **Rows 4–5, 8–9, 12–13, 16–17, 20–21, 24–25, 28–29,** and **32–33** in cool colors (that is, OB, NB, DG, LG, BG, MB, PU, and SG) and **Rows 6–7, 10–11, 14–15, 18–19, 22–23, 26–27, 30–31,** and **34–35** in warm colors (that is, BE, E, DO, G, DR, PE, MA, and BR) in any arrangement you like, drawing inspiration from the photo.

2. Assemble the motifs into a 6-by-6 square using overcast stitch (see page 9).

3. For the inner border, work 2 rows of dc in dark red around the entire edge. Then work 77 rectangles of different widths, all 8 rows of double crochet high, around the edge. See the table below for the colors used (the blocks go in numerical order all the way around). Sew the sides of the rectangles together with overcast stitch (see diagram).

Border Colors Shown

1, 11, 46	MB
2, 18, 36, 50, 54, 62	OB
3, 12, 24, 39, 56	SG
4, 15, 32, 40, 64	BE
5, 14, 28, 33, 38, 65, 68	NB
6, 21, 25, 52, 66	SB
7, 19, 37, 41, 67	BR
8, 17, 35, 43, 55, 69	E
9, 20, 27, 51, 61	DO
10, 16, 22, 30, 53, 63	LG
13, 47, 57, 73, 77	G
26, 42, 59, 71, 74	MA
23, 34, 44, 58, 70	PE
31, 45, 60, 72, 75	PU
29, 49	DG
48, 76	BG

4. For the outer border, work 2 rounds of double crochet, then 1 round shell pattern (see diagram) around the edge in dark red.

Square Motif

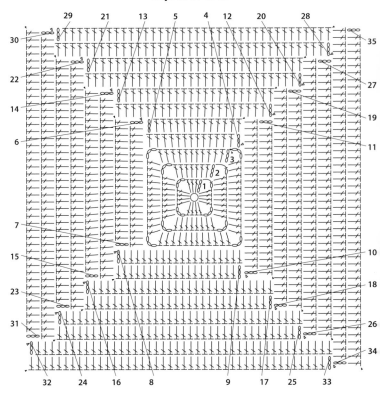

❖ For how to change colors, see page 9.

◄ cut the yarn   ◁ join the yarn

Borders

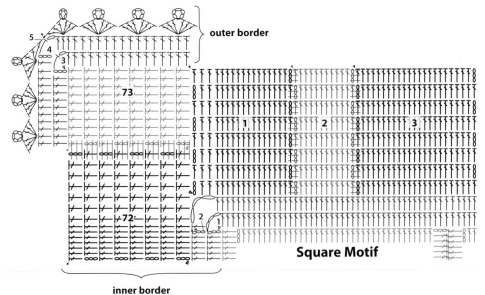

outer border

inner border

Square Motif

1, 2, 3 . . . Sunflowers!

A few well-chosen prints for the centers, borders crocheted in the round for the petals, and a filler motif to make in a range of varied tones—that's all there is to it!

Materials

- 3.5 oz./100 g #4 medium weight cotton yarn in the following colors: ecru, beige, brown, orange, light pink, and black
- Various coordinating print fabrics
- Quilt batting
- US E-4 (3.5 mm) crochet hook (or size needed to obtain gauge)

Gauge

1 filler motif = 9 by 9 in. (22 by 22 cm)

Measurements

See diagram below.

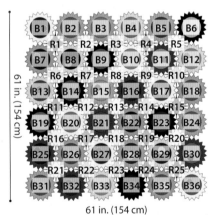

61 in. (154 cm)

61 in. (154 cm)

Instructions

1. Ch 120 and join with a sl st to form a ring. Work the border rounds as shown in the diagram at right. Make 36 borders in this way. For the colors, see the table opposite.

Border Colors Shown

B1, B10, B17, B20, B27, B36	ecru
B2, B5, B15, B24, B28, B31	beige
B3, B7, B18, B22, B26, B35	orange
B4, B8, B12, B13, B29, B33	pink
B6, B9, B14, B19, B23, B34	black
B11, B16, B21, B25, B30, B32	brown

2. Starting with the second border, attach each motif to the previous one(s) with sc in the ch-sps of the final round as shown in the diagram. Make 6 rows of 6 borders each.

Border

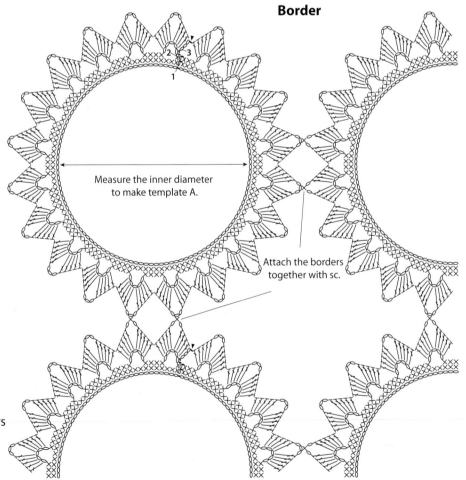

Measure the inner diameter to make template A.

Attach the borders together with sc.

Colorful Crochet Afghans and Pillows

1, 2, 3 . . . Sunflowers!

3. Make 25 filler motifs (for the colors used, see the table below), attaching them in the spaces between the borders with single crochets as you work the last round.

Filler Motif

Filler Colors Shown

F2, F5, F13, F20, F21	ecru
F3, F6, F10, F14, F22	beige
F7, F9, F23	orange
F8, F12, F16, F18	pink
F1, F4, F17, F25	black
F11, F15, F19, F24	brown

4. Measure the inner diameter of the border motifs and draw a circle with that diameter on a piece of stiff paper. Cut this piece out; it will be **template A**. See "Making the Fabric Circles" on page 39.

Making the Fabric Circles

Using **template A**, cut out 72 circles from different fabrics, adding a seam allowance of ⅜ in. (1 cm) all the way around the edge.

Cut **template A** out of the quilt batting 36 times, adding a seam allowance of ¼ in. (0.5 cm) around the edge.

Place 2 fabric circles together, right sides together, and place a batting circle on top. Sew all the way around the edge. Make a cut 2 in. (5 cm) long in one of the fabric circles and use this opening to turn the piece right side out, so the batting is on the inside. Sew the opening closed with invisible stitches. Cut round patches from the remnants of fabric and appliqué them over the closed openings to hide them.

5. Blind stitch the fabric circles inside the crocheted borders.

Nine-Patch Quilt with 3-D Flowers

With its flashy color palette and the playful flowers, this afghan evokes the happy era of the sixties and seventies.

Materials

- 1.75 oz./50 g #1 super fine weight cotton yarn in the following colors: dark blue, magenta, pink, coral, ivory, and dark red
- 3.5 oz./100 g #1 super fine weight cotton yarn in the following colors: light blue, turquoise, sky blue, red, and lime green
- US E-4 (3.5 mm) crochet hook (or size needed to obtain gauge)

Nine-Patch Quilt with 3-D Flowers

Gauge

1 motif B = 6 by 6 in. (16.5 by 16.5 cm)

Measurements

See diagram below.

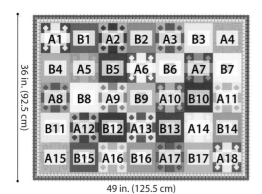

Instructions

1. Starting with a magic loop, crochet the **a1** and **a2** motifs for **motif A** as shown in the diagrams. For the colors used, see the table at right.

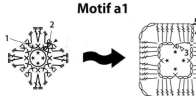

Motif a1   ### Motif a2

Work the single crochets of Round 3 through the unworked back loops of the stitches of Round 1.

❖ For how to change colors, see page 9.

△ join the yarn   ◄ cut the yarn

Ī Ī ⋉ **Stitches worked through the front loop:** Work the stitch indicated (sc, hdc, or dc), inserting the hook through the *front loop only* of the stitch of the previous round.

2. Assemble the motifs, alternating **a1** and **a2**, with overcast stitch (see page 9).

Motif A

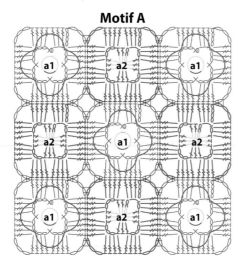

Motif A Colors Shown

	a1 Motifs	a2 Motifs
A1	Rnds 1–2: sky blue Rnds 3–4: dark blue	sky blue
A2	Rnds 1–2: dark red Rnds 3–4: red	dark red
A3	Rnds 1–2: red Rnds 3–4: lime green	red
A4	Rnds 1–2: lime green Rnds 3–4: pink	lime green
A5	Rnds 1–2: lime green Rnds 3–4: coral	lime green
A6	Rnds 1–2: ivory Rnds 3–4: magenta	ivory
A7	Rnds 1–2: turquoise Rnds 3–4: dark blue	turquoise
A8	Rnds 1–2: red Rnds 3–4: coral	red
A9	Rnds 1–2: turquoise Rnds 3–4: light blue	turquoise
A10	Rnds 1–2: pink Rnds 3–4: magenta	pink
A11	Rnds 1–2: lime green Rnds 3–4: light blue	lime green
A12	Rnds 1–2: dark blue Rnds 3–4: lime green	dark blue
A13	Rnds 1–2: red Rnds 3–4: light blue	red
A14	Rnds 1–2: ivory Rnds 3–4: light blue	ivory
A15	Rnds 1–2: pink Rnds 3–4: lime green	pink
A16	Rnds 1–2: lime green Rnds 3–4: light blue	lime green
A17	Rnds 1–2: magenta Rnds 3–4: turquoise	magenta
A18	Rnds 1–2: light blue Rnds 3–4: red	light blue

Nine-Patch Quilt with 3-D Flowers

3. Work **motif B** in the colors indicated in the chart.

Motif B

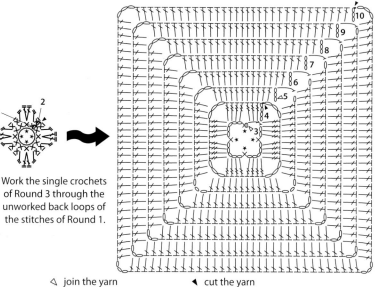

Work the single crochets of Round 3 through the unworked back loops of the stitches of Round 1.

◁ join the yarn   ◀ cut the yarn

Stitches worked through the front loop: Work the stitch indicated (sc, hdc, or dc), inserting the hook through the *front loop only* of the stitch of the previous round.

Motif B Colors Shown

	Rnds 1–2	Rnds 3–4	Rnds 5–10
B1	coral	light blue	magenta
B2	dark blue	lime green	turquoise
B3	red	lime green	light blue
B4	turquoise	lime green	pink
B5	red	lime green	dark blue
B6	light blue	dark red	light blue
B7	red	magenta	ivory
B8	pink	lime green	ivory
B9	red	dark blue	lime green
B10	lime green	dark blue	dark red
B11	coral	magenta	light blue
B12	lime green	light blue	dark red
B13	dark red	coral	dark blue
B14	dark blue	ivory	coral
B15	dark blue	ivory	red
B16	magenta	ivory	coral
B17	lime green	coral	lime green

4. Assemble the motifs, alternating **A** and **B**, with overcast stitch (see page 9).

5. For the border, work 2 rounds in lime green, then 2 rounds in sky blue, then 2 rounds of turquoise, and finally 2 rounds of red as shown in the diagram opposite.

Assembly and Border

border

B1

B4

Work the dc in the corresponding stitch 2 rounds below, working over the ch of the previous round.

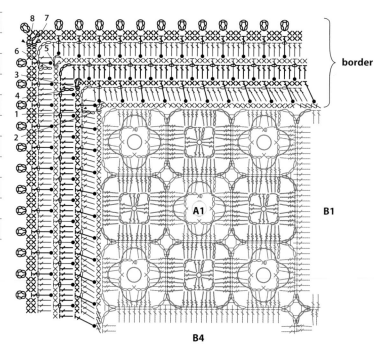

Around the World

Around the World

A beautiful exercise in style, this generously sized afghan consists of a single flower worked 441 times in a superb gradient of hues moving from pink to violet.

Materials

- #3 light weight merino wool yarn in the following colors: 1.75 oz./50 g pink (**P**), 3.5 oz./100 g old rose (**OR**), 5.25 oz./150 g beige (**BE**), 5.25 oz./150 g brown (**BR**), 7 oz./200 g coral (**C**), 7 oz./200 g red (**R**), 10.5 oz./300 g dark red (**DR**), 10.5 oz./300 g magenta (**MG**), 12.25 oz./350 g maroon (**MR**), 14 oz./400 g violet (**V**), 14 oz./400 g mulberry (**MU**), and 3.5 oz./100 g mauve (**MV**)
- US E-4 (3.5 mm) crochet hook (or size needed to obtain gauge)

Gauge

1 motif = 3 by 3 in. (8 by 8 cm)

Measurements

See diagram below.

Assembly

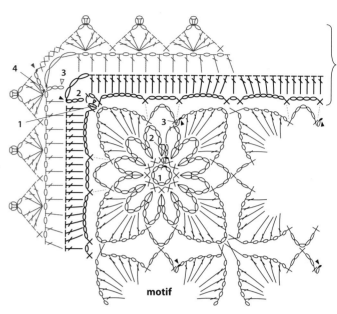

border

motif

◀ cut the yarn

△ join the yarn

▽ **Cluster:** *Yarn over, insert the hook through the stitch, yarn over, pull up a loop; repeat from * 3 times in the same stitch, then yarn over and pull the yarn through all the loops on the hook.

Instructions

1. Starting with a ring of 8 chains, work the motif as shown in the diagram above.

2. For the colors used, see the diagram opposite.

3. Starting with the second motif, join each motif to the previous motif(s) with single crochet as shown in the diagram above. Make 441 motifs (which will be 21 rows of 21 motifs).

4. For the border, work 1 round of single crochet and chains and 1 round of double crochet in mauve, then 1 round of double crochet and chains and 1 round of shells in mulberry; see the diagram above.

69 in. (176 cm)

69 in. (176 cm)

P	OR	BE	BR	C	R	DR	MG	MR	V	MU	V	MR	MG	DR	R	C	BR	BE	OR	P
OR	BE	BR	C	R	DR	MG	MR	V	MU	V	MU	V	MR	MG	DR	R	C	BR	BE	OR
BE	BR	C	R	DR	MG	MR	V	MU	V	MR	V	MU	V	MR	MG	DR	R	C	BR	BE
BR	C	R	DR	MG	MR	V	MU	V	MR	MG	MR	V	MU	V	MR	MG	DR	R	C	BR
C	R	DR	MG	MR	V	MU	V	MR	MG	DR	MG	MR	V	MU	V	MR	MG	DR	R	C
R	DR	MG	MR	V	MU	V	MR	MG	DR	R	DR	MG	MR	V	MU	V	MR	MG	DR	R
DR	MG	MR	V	MU	V	MR	MG	DR	R	C	R	DR	MG	MR	V	MU	V	MR	MG	DR
MG	MR	V	MU	V	MR	MG	DR	R	C	BR	C	R	DR	MG	MR	V	MU	V	MR	MG
MR	V	MU	V	MR	MG	DR	R	C	BR	BE	BR	C	R	DR	MG	MR	V	MU	V	MR
V	MU	V	MR	MG	DR	R	C	BR	BE	OR	BE	BR	C	R	DR	MG	MR	V	MU	V
MU	V	MR	MG	DR	R	C	BR	BE	OR	P	OR	BE	BR	C	R	DR	MG	MR	V	MU
V	MU	V	MR	MG	DR	R	C	BR	BE	OR	BE	BR	C	R	DR	MG	MR	V	MU	V
MR	V	MU	V	MR	MG	DR	R	C	BR	BE	BR	C	R	DR	MG	MR	V	MU	V	MR
MG	MR	V	MU	V	MR	MG	DR	R	C	BR	C	R	DR	MG	MR	V	MU	V	MR	MG
DR	MG	MR	V	MU	V	MR	MG	DR	R	C	R	DR	MG	MR	V	MU	V	MR	MG	DR
R	DR	MG	MR	V	MU	V	MR	MG	DR	R	DR	MG	MR	V	MU	V	MR	MG	DR	R
C	R	DR	MG	MR	V	MU	V	MR	MG	DR	MG	MR	V	MU	V	MR	MG	DR	R	C
BR	C	R	DR	MG	MR	V	MU	V	MR	MG	MR	V	MU	V	MR	MG	DR	R	C	BR
BE	BR	C	R	DR	MG	MR	V	MU	V	MR	V	MU	V	MR	MG	DR	R	C	BR	BE
OR	BE	BR	C	R	DR	MG	MR	V	MU	V	MU	V	MR	MG	DR	R	C	BR	BE	OR
P	OR	BE	BR	C	R	DR	MG	MR	V	MU	V	MR	MG	DR	R	C	BR	BE	OR	P

Hexagon Mosaic

In the style of a scrap quilt, everything here rests on the variety of colors, which will yield surprising combinations while establishing a harmony through the whole piece.

Materials

- 1.75 oz./50 g each in a range of 23 colors of #1 super fine wool yarn (shown in Fine Tweed by Rowan)
- US E-4 (3.5 mm) crochet hook (or size needed to obtain gauge)

Gauge

1 motif = 6 by 7 in. (15 by 18.5 cm)

Measurements

See diagram below.

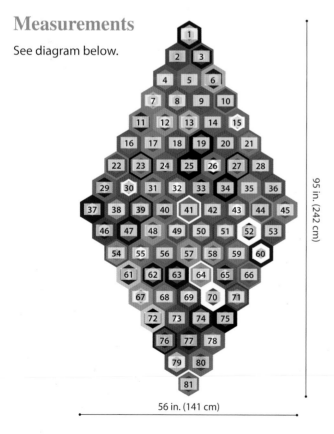

95 in. (242 cm)

56 in. (141 cm)

Hexagon Mosaic

Instructions

1. Ch 6 and join into a ring with a sl st. Work the motifs as shown in the diagram.

3. Assemble the motifs with overcast stitch (see page 9).

Motif

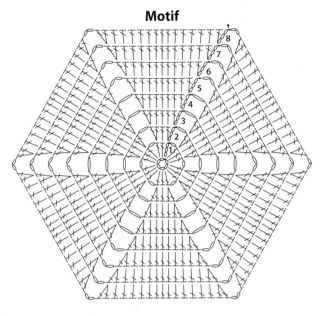

Assembly

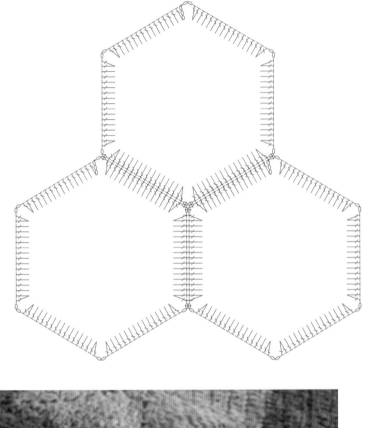

❖ For how to change colors, see page 9.

◀ cut the yarn   ◁ join the yarn

2. Make 81 motifs, changing the colors randomly.

Note: Don't use more than 4 different colors in each motif.

Childhood Neons

Childhood Neons

This variation on hexagon motifs includes 50 hues arranged in a gradient and surrounded with yellow and green in candy colors.

Materials

- Small amounts of #1 super fine weight cotton yarn in 50 colors [shown in DMC Soft Cotton No. 4 (Art 89)]
- #1 super fine weight cotton yarn in ivory (3.5 oz./100 g), light green (3.5 oz./100 g), and yellow (5.25 oz./150 g) (shown in DMC Fil Natura in Ivory, Bamboo, and Sunflower)
- US C-2 or D-3 (3.0 mm) crochet hook (or size needed to obtain gauge)

Gauge

1 motif = 4 by 4½ in. (10 by 11.5 cm)

Measurements

See diagram at right.

Instructions

1. Work the motifs as shown in the diagram below, starting with a ring of 6 chs joined with a sl st.

2. Make 50 motifs. For the colors used, see the table below.

Colors Shown

Rnd 1	ivory
Rnds 2–3	any color
Rnd 4	ivory
Rnd 5	yellow
Rnd 6	light green

3. Assemble the motifs in 9 staggered rows of 5 or 6 motifs each with overcast stitch (see page 9) as shown in the diagram below.

4. For the border, work 1 round of double crochet in light green and 1 round of double crochet and popcorn stitch in yellow, as shown in the diagram.

Ch 4, in 4th ch from hook work **1 popcorn stitch** (6 dc, stretch out loop and remove from hook, insert hook through first dc from front to back, pick loop up again and pull through first stitch, pulling on the working yarn to pull tight); ch 4, sl st in first ch.

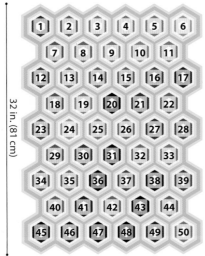

Motif

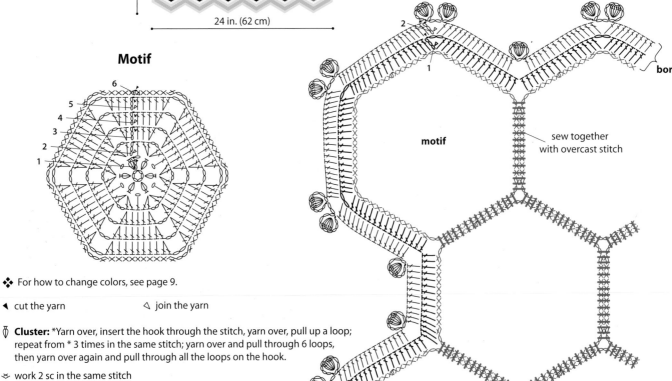

Assembly

border

motif

sew together with overcast stitch

❖ For how to change colors, see page 9.

◄ cut the yarn   ◁ join the yarn

Cluster: *Yarn over, insert the hook through the stitch, yarn over, pull up a loop; repeat from * 3 times in the same stitch; yarn over and pull through 6 loops, then yarn over again and pull through all the loops on the hook.

⤳ work 2 sc in the same stitch

Fans

Light beige and ivory come together with brown and blue to produce a perfect, muted harmony in this small afghan with a picot border that speaks of a sweet life.

Materials

- 3.5 oz./100 g #3 light weight 100% linen yarn (shown in Katia Linen) in the following colors: deep blue, navy blue, gray blue, ivory, beige, dark beige, and brown
- US E-4 (3.5 mm) crochet hook (or size needed to obtain gauge)

Gauge

1 motif **A** = 5¾ by 5¾ in. (14.5 by 14.5 cm)

Measurements

See diagram below.

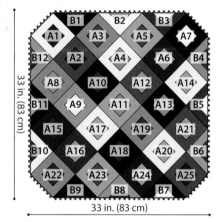

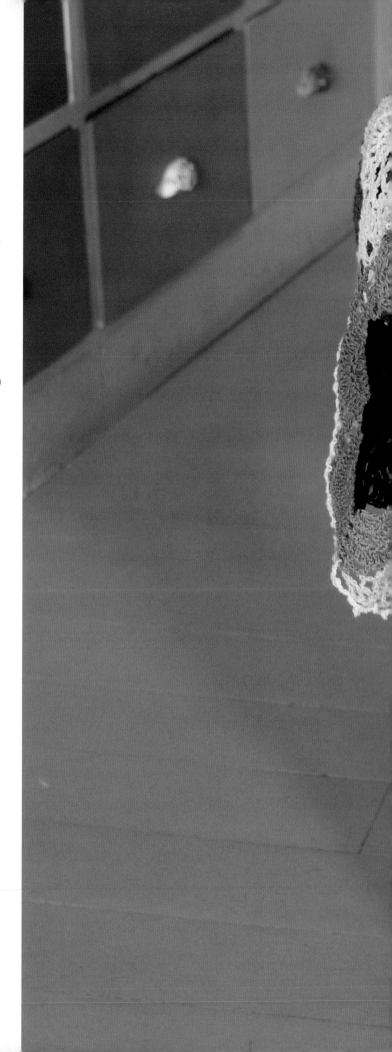

Fans

Instructions

1. Ch 6 and join with a sl st to form a ring, then continue with **motif A** as shown in the diagram below.

2. Use any color you choose for Rnds. 1–5 and another color of your choice for Rnds. 6–10. Make 25 **motif As**, attaching each one to the previous motifs with sl sts as you work the final round (see assembly diagram below); follow the numerical order shown in the diagram on page 54 (first make A1, then A2, A3, etc.)

3. Crochet 12 **motif Bs** (see diagram below) in any colors you choose and attach them to the **motif As** with sl sts as you work the final round, as before.

4. For the border, work as shown in the diagram below.

Motif A

Motif B

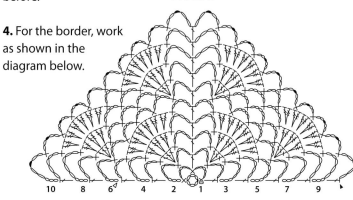

❖ For how to change colors, see page 9.

◄ cut the yarn   △ join the yarn

Assembly

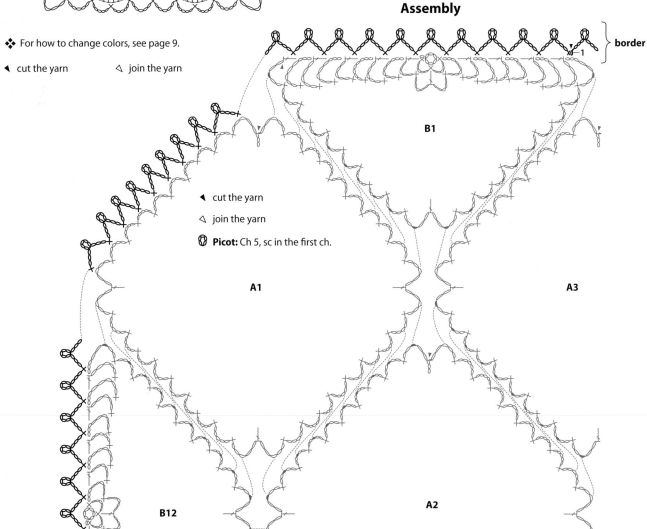

◄ cut the yarn

△ join the yarn

🔘 **Picot:** Ch 5, sc in the first ch.

Tutti Frutti Granny Squares

In berry, mint, or tropical fruit color schemes, these four gradient pillow designs will wake up tired couches and armchairs.

GENERAL INSTRUCTIONS FOR ALL 4 PILLOWS

Gauge

Rnds 1–3 = 2½ by 2½ in. (6.5 by 6.5 cm)

Instructions

1. Follow the diagram below, starting with a magic loop. Change colors as indicated in the instructions for each pillow (for the colors used, see table under each pattern).

first border round

The number of rounds varies between the pillows.

❖ For how to change colors, see page 9.

◀ cut the yarn   ◁ join the yarn

⚛ work 3 scs in the same st

2. For the border, work 1 round of dc in black, then 1 round of sc in red, then 1 more round of dc in black, as shown in the diagram.

3. Make a pillow cover from the fabric (see page 5) and blind stitch the crocheted part to the front.

PINK-TO-VIOLET GRADIENT PILLOW

Materials

- Scrap amounts of #1 super fine weight wool yarn in the following colors: pink, magenta, raspberry, mauve, dark mauve, plum, lavender, black, and red
- Matching fabric, 18 by 43 in. (45 by 110 cm)
- US E-4 (3.5 mm) crochet hook (or size needed to obtain gauge)

Measurements

See diagram.

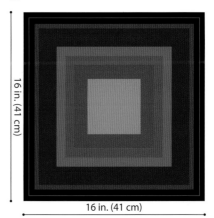

16 in. (41 cm)   16 in. (41 cm)

Colors Shown

Rnds 1–6	pink
Rnds 7–9	magenta
Rnds 10–11	raspberry
Rnds 12–13	mauve
Rnds 14–15	dark mauve
Rnds 16–18	plum
Rnd 19	lavender

Tutti Frutti Granny Squares

BLUE-TO-GREEN GRADIENT PILLOW

Materials

- Scrap amounts of #1 super fine weight wool yarn in the following colors: light blue, medium blue, forest green, olive green, khaki, leaf green, mint green, black, and red
- Matching fabric, 20 by 43 in. (50 by 110 cm)
- US E-4 (3.5 mm) crochet hook (or size needed to obtain gauge)

Measurements

See diagram.

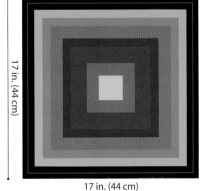

17 in. (44 cm)

17 in. (44 cm)

Colors Shown

Rnds 1–3	light blue
Rnds 4–7	medium blue
Rnds 8–12	forest green
Rnds 13–14	olive green
Rnds 15–17	khaki
Rnds 18–19	leaf green
Rnds 20–21	mint green

PURPLE-TO-BLUE GRADIENT PILLOW

Materials

- Scrap amounts of #1 super fine weight wool yarn in the following colors: purple, gray-blue, navy blue, medium blue, light blue, black, and red
- Matching fabric, 18 by 43 in. (45 by 110 cm)
- US E-4 (3.5 mm) crochet hook (or size needed to obtain gauge)

Measurements

See diagram.

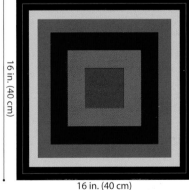

16 in. (40 cm)

16 in. (40 cm)

Colors Shown

Rnds 1–6	purple
Rnds 7–9	gray-blue
Rnds 10–14	navy blue
Rnds 15–17	medium blue
Rnds 18–19	light blue

Tutti Frutti Granny Squares

YELLOW-TO-MAROON GRADIENT

Materials

- Scrap amounts of #1 super fine weight wool yarn in the following colors: ivory, warm gray, dark khaki, beige, mustard yellow, khaki, orange, pink, maroon, black, and red
- Matching fabric, 24 by 47 in. (60 by 120 cm)
- US E-4 (3.5 mm) crochet hook (or size needed to obtain gauge)

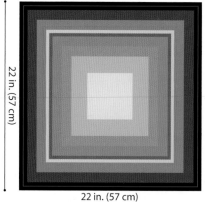

22 in. (57 cm)

22 in. (57 cm)

Measurements

See diagram.

Colors Shown

Rnds 1–9	ivory
Rnds 10–14	warm gray
Rnds 15–17	beige
Rnds 18–20	khaki
Rnd 21	dark khaki
Rnd 22	mustard yellow
Rnds 23	orange
Rnds 24–25	pink
Rnds 26–27	maroon

Fan Variation

Fan Variation

Here's a project every crocheter dreams of—a chance to use up your remnants of yarn and try out daring color combinations.

Materials

- Scrap amounts of #1 super fine weight wool yarn in the following colors: old rose, medium blue, orange, lime green, mint green, yellow, magenta, mauve, and light blue
- Matching fabric, 24 by 47 in. (60 by 120 cm)
- US E-4 (3.5 mm) crochet hook (or size needed to obtain gauge)

Gauge

1 motif = 10 by 10 in. (24.5 by 24.5 cm)

Measurements

See diagram below.

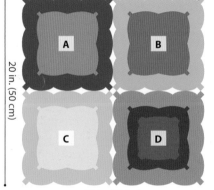

20 in. (50 cm)

20 in. (50 cm)

Motif

❖ For how to change colors, see page 9.

◀ cut the yarn

◁ join the yarn

Assembly

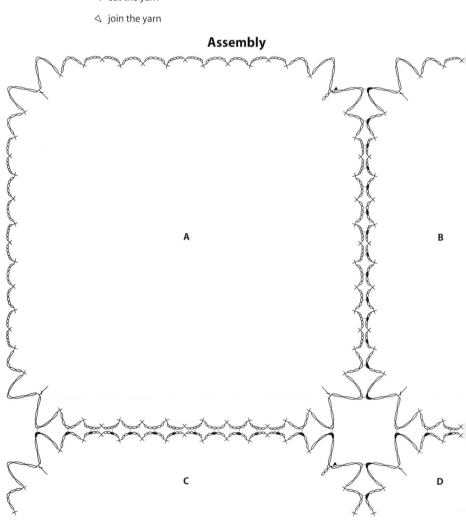

Instructions

1. Ch 6 and join with a sl st to form a ring, then work the motif as shown in the diagram.

2. For the color changes, see the table below.

Work the 4 motifs, joining each one to the previous motif(s) with sl st as you work the last round (see the assembly diagram on page 66).

3. Make a pillow cover from the fabric (see page 5) and blind stitch the crocheted part to the front.

Colors Shown

Rounds	Motif A	Motif B	Motif C	Rounds	Motif D
Rnds 1–10	old rose	orange	mint green	Rnds 1–6	magenta
Rnds 11–14	medium blue	lime green	yellow	Rnds 7–10	mauve
				Rnds 11–14	light blue

Bohemian

We love granny squares—so make as many as you want!

Materials

- Scrap amounts of #1 super fine weight wool yarn in the following colors: beige-mustard, coral, purple, mint green, magenta, medium blue, forest green, brown, old rose, sky blue, straw, bright orange, dark khaki, fuchsia, dark blue, mustard yellow, dark beige, and plum
- Matching fabric, 18 by 43 in. (45 by 110 cm)
- US E-4 (3.5 mm) crochet hook (or size needed to obtain gauge)

Gauge

1 motif = 7 by 7 in. (17.5 by 17.5 cm)

Measurements

See diagram.

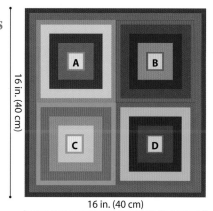

16 in. (40 cm)

16 in. (40 cm)

Instructions

1. Starting with a magic loop, work the motif as shown in the diagram opposite.

2. Make 4 motifs. For the colors used, see the table on page 69.

3. Working from the back of the work, attach motif **A** and motif **B** together with a row of single crochet. Do the same with motifs **C** and **D**. Then attach halves **A/B** and **C/D** together in the same way.

4. For the border, work 2 rounds of double crochet and chains in dark beige around the edge of the entire piece, then 1 round of double crochet in plum, as shown in the diagram opposite.

5. Make a pillow cover from the fabric (see page 5) and blind sew the crocheted part to the front.

Motif

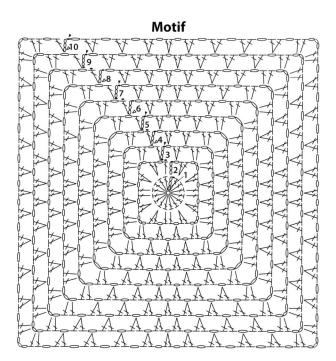

❖ For how to change colors, see page 9.

Assembly

A   B

C   D

border

◀ cut the yarn

◁ join the yarn

Colors Shown

Rounds	Motif A	Motif B
Rnds 1–3	beige-mustard	magenta
Rnds 4–5	coral	medium blue
Rnds 6–7	purple	forest green
Rnds 8–9	mint green	brown
Rnd 10	beige-mustard	magenta

Rounds	Motif C	Motif D
Rnds 1–3	old rose	dark khaki
Rnds 4–5	sky blue	fuchsia
Rnds 6–7	straw	dark blue
Rnds 8–9	bright orange	mustard yellow
Rnd 10	old rose	dark khaki

Light and Shadow

A subtle play of negative and positive space around a simple central flower—intriguing and captivating.

Materials

- 1.75 oz./50 g #1 super fine weight cotton yarn in the following colors: black, pale pink, light purple, violet, and plum
- Matching fabric, 18 by 43 in. (45 by 110 cm)
- US E-4 (3.5 mm) crochet hook (or size needed to obtain gauge)

Gauge

Rnds 1–3 = 2¾ by 2¾ in. (7 by 7 cm)

Measurements

See diagram.

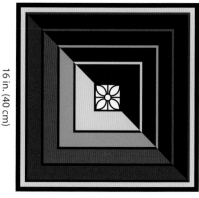

16 in. (40 cm)

16 in. (40 cm)

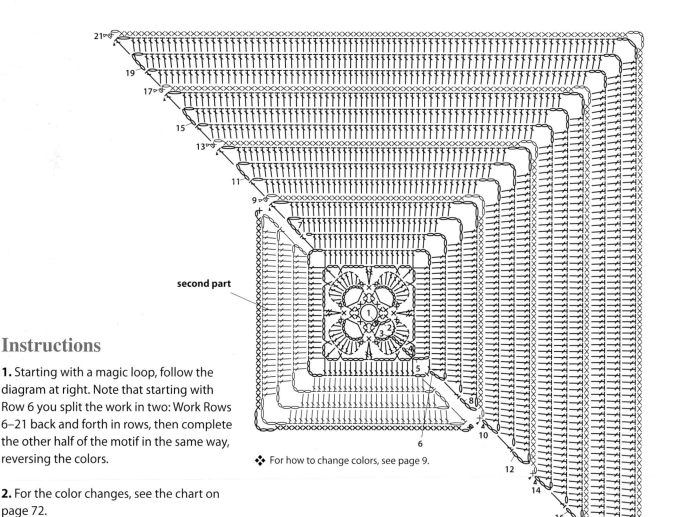

second part

Instructions

1. Starting with a magic loop, follow the diagram at right. Note that starting with Row 6 you split the work in two: Work Rows 6–21 back and forth in rows, then complete the other half of the motif in the same way, reversing the colors.

2. For the color changes, see the chart on page 72.

❖ For how to change colors, see page 9.

Light and Shadow

Color Pattern

Rnds 1–5	black
Rows 6–8	half black, half pale pink
Row 9	half pale pink, half black
Rows 10–12	half black, half light purple
Row 13	half light purple, half black
Rows 14–16	half black, half violet
Row 17	half violet, half black
Rows 18–20	half black, half plum
Row 21	half plum, half black

3. Attach the two halves of the motif together with overcast stitch (see page 9).

4. For the border, work 1 round of double crochet around the edge in pale pink, then 1 round in black, as shown in the diagram below.

5. Make a pillow cover from the fabric (see page 5) and blind stitch the crocheted part to the front.

border

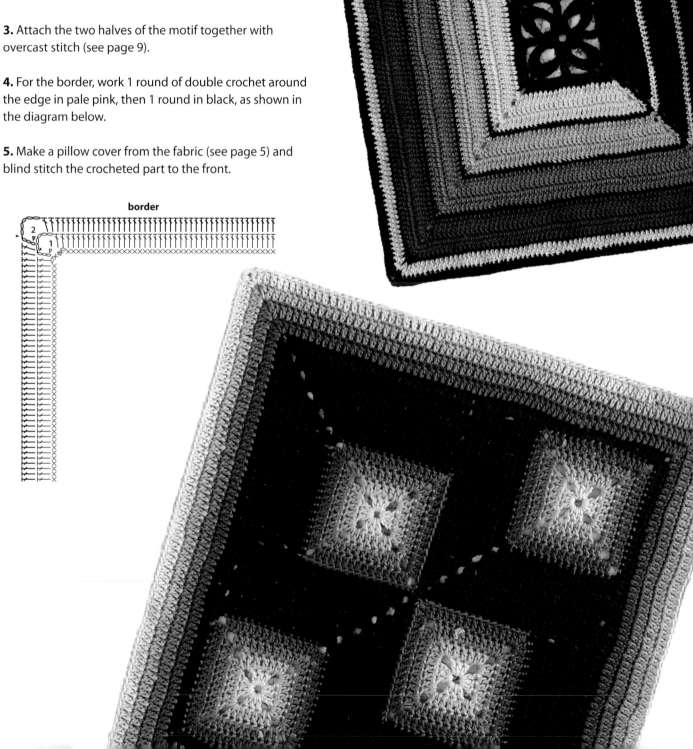

Gradient Squares

Made in the same shades as the previous project, this pillow offers a different but complementary interpretation.

Materials

- 1.75 oz./50 g #1 super fine weight cotton yarn in the following colors: pale pink, light purple, violet, plum, and black
- Matching fabric, 18 by 43 in. (45 by 110 cm)
- US E-4 (3.5 mm) crochet hook (or size needed to obtain gauge)

Gauge

1 motif = 5½ by 5½ in. (14 by 14 cm)

Measurements

See diagram.

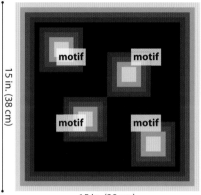

15 in. (38 cm)

15 in. (38 cm)

Instructions

1. Work a motif as shown in the diagram below, starting with a magic loop.

2. For the color pattern, see the table below. Crochet 4 motifs following this pattern.

Color Pattern

Rnd 1	light pink
Rnd 2	light purple
Rnd 3	violet
Rnd 4	plum
Rows 5–9 (on 2 sides only)	black

3. Assemble the motifs together into a square with overcast stitch (see page 9) in black.

4. For the border, work 1 round of double crochet around the whole edge in black, then 1 round in plum, 1 round in violet, 1 round in light purple, and 1 round in pale pink, as shown in the diagram below.

5. Make a pillow cover from the fabric (see page 5) and blind stitch the crocheted part to the front.

Assembly

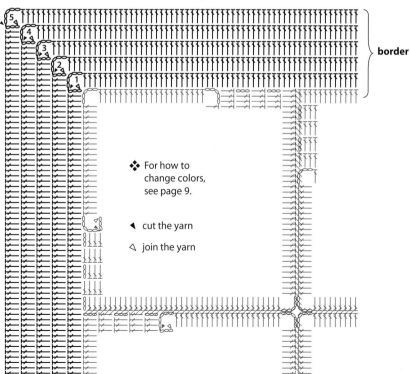

border

❖ For how to change colors, see page 9.

◀ cut the yarn

△ join the yarn

Motif

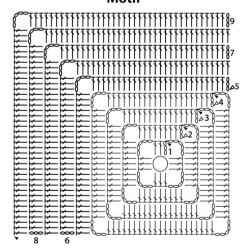

Playing with Stripes

Pull out your stash of scraps from previous projects and crochet these lovely stripes in marguerite stitch for a guaranteed vintage look!

Materials

- Scrap amounts of #1 super fine weight wool yarn in the following colors: raspberry, off-white, forest green, dark red, magenta, dark blue, dark lavender, red, blue gray, beige, khaki, old rose, lime green, sky blue, brown, dark orange, light purple, plum, pink, teal, light yellow, dark brown, light blue, orange, turquoise, maroon, blue, mint green, light green, yellow, coral, and black
- Matching fabric, 24 by 47 in. (60 by 120 cm)
- US E-4 (3.5 mm) crochet hook (or size needed to obtain gauge)

Gauge

1 motif = 6 by 6 in. (16 by 16 cm)

Measurements

See diagram.

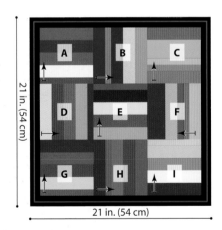

21 in. (54 cm)

21 in. (54 cm)

⊢→ direction of work

Instructions

1. Starting with a foundation chain of 31 chs, crochet the motifs as shown in the diagram below.

Motif

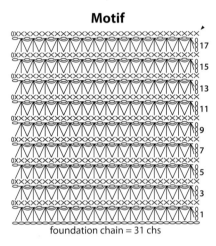

foundation chain = 31 chs

❖ For how to change colors, see page 9.

Marguerite stitch: Ch 3, turn. Insert the hook in the 2nd chain, yarn over, and pull up a loop; insert the hook in the 3rd chain, yarn over, and pull up a loop; [insert the hook into the next stitch, yarn over, and pull up a loop] twice; yarn over, pull through all 5 loops on the hook; ch 1. *Insert the hook into the center of the marguerite stitch just made, yarn over, pull up a loop; insert the hook into the same stitch as the last leg of the marguerite stitch just made, yarn over, pull up a loop; [insert the hook into the next stitch, yarn over, and pull up a loop] twice; yarn over, pull through all 5 loops on the hook; ch 1. Repeat from * across the row.

Playing with Stripes

2. For the colors used, see the table below. Crochet motifs A through I.

Colors Shown

Rows	A
Rows 1–2	raspberry
Rows 3–6	off-white
Rows 7–10	forest green
Rows 11–14	dark red
Rows 15–18	magenta

Rows	B
Rows 1–4	dark blue
Rows 5–6	dark lavender
Rows 7–10	maroon
Rows 11–14	blue gray
Rows 15–18	beige

Rows	C
Rows 1–4	light purple
Rows 5–6	khaki
Rows 7–8	old rose
Rows 9–14	lime green
Rows 15–18	raspberry

Rows	D
Rows 1–4	sky blue
Rows 5–8	brown
Rows 9–12	dark orange
Rows 13–16	light purple
Rows 17–18	plum

Rows	E
Rows 1–4	pink
Rows 5–8	teal
Rows 9–12	light yellow
Rows 13–16	dark brown
Rows 17–18	red

Rows	F
Rows 1–4	old rose
Rows 5–6	orange
Rows 7–8	forest green
Rows 9–12	light blue
Rows 13–18	plum

Rows	G
Rows 1–2	forest green
Rows 3–6	light green
Rows 7–10	turquoise
Rows 11–14	magenta
Rows 15–16	plum
Rows 17–18	maroon

Rows	H
Rows 1–4	plum
Rows 5–6	dark orange
Rows 7–10	blue
Rows 11–14	brown
Rows 15–18	forest green

Rows	I
Rows 1–4	plum
Rows 5–8	off-white
Rows 9–12	coral
Rows 13–16	mint green
Rows 17–18	yellow

3. Assemble the motifs in a 3-by-3 square with overcast stitch (see page 9), going through only one strand of each stitch.

4. For the border, work 2 rounds of double crochet around the whole edge in black, then 1 round of single crochet in red, then 2 more rounds of double crochet in black, as shown in the diagram below.

5. Make a pillow cover from the fabric (see page 5) and blind stitch the crocheted part to the front.

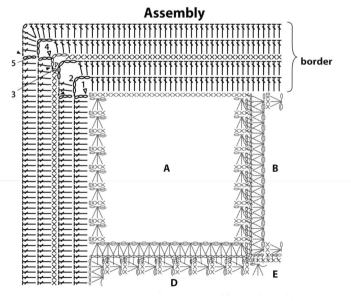

Assembly

◄ cut the yarn   ◁ join the yarn

Nine-Patch Pillow
with 3-D Flowers

Nine-Patch Pillow with 3-D Flowers

Based on the same design as the afghan on page 40, this pillow creates pleasant surprises with unexpected color harmonies.

Materials

- Scrap amounts of wool yarn in the following colors: magenta, royal blue, orange, red, pink, plum, yellow, coral, lime green, mint green, white, and black
- Matching fabric, 24 by 47 in. (60 by 120 cm)
- US E-4 (3.5 mm) crochet hook (or size needed to obtain gauge)

Gauge

1 motif B = 6 by 6 in. (16.5 by 16.5 cm)

Measurements

See diagram below.

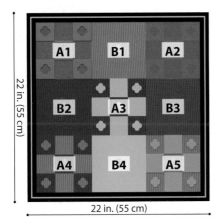

Instructions

1. Starting with a magic loop, work the **a1** and **a2** motifs for **motif A** as shown in the diagrams. For the colors used, see the table, above right.

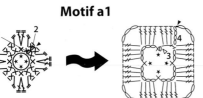

Work the single crochets of Round 3 through the unworked back loops of the stitches of Round 1.

❖ For how to change colors, see page 9.

Colors Shown—Motif A

	a1 Motifs	a2 Motifs
A1	Rnds 1–2: magenta Rnds 3–4: royal blue	magenta
A2	Rnds 1–2: red Rnds 3–4: magenta	red
A3	Rnds 1–2: yellow Rnds 3–4: plum	yellow
A4	Rnds 1–2: orange Rnds 3–4: plum	coral
A5	Rnds 1–2: mint green Rnds 3–4: orange	mint green

2. Assemble the motifs, alternating **a1** and **a2**, with overcast stitch (see page 9).

Motif A

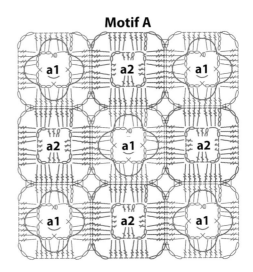

◀ cut the yarn   △ join the yarn

⊤ ⊤ ⊼ **Stitches worked through the front loop:** Work the stitch indicated (sc, hdc, or dc), inserting the hook through the *front loop only* of the stitch of the previous round.

Colors Shown—Motif B

B1	Rnds 1–2: white Rnds 3–10: orange
B2	Rnds 1–2: red Rnds 3–10: pink
B3	Rnds 1–2: plum Rnds 3–10: coral
B4	Rnds 1–2: magenta Rnds 3–10: lime green

3. Work **motif B** 4 times. For the colors used, see the chart on page 78.

Motif B

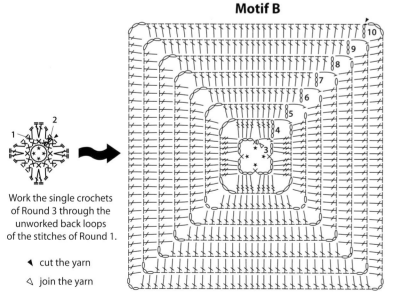

Work the single crochets of Round 3 through the unworked back loops of the stitches of Round 1.

◄ cut the yarn

△ join the yarn

4. Assemble the **A** and **B** motifs with overcast stitch (see page 9).

5. For the border, work 1 round of double crochet around the edge in black, then 1 round of single crochet in yellow, then another round of double crochet in black, as shown in the diagram below.

6. Make a pillow cover from the fabric (see page 5) and blind stitch the crocheted part to the front.

Assembly

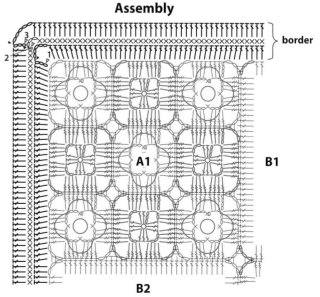

Originally published as *Crochet Country*, Kristel Salgarollo
Copyright © Les Éditions de Saxe 2014
www.edisaxe.com

First published in the U.S.A. by Stackpole Books in 2015.
STACKPOLE BOOKS
5067 Ritter Road
Mechanicsburg, PA 17055
www.stackpolebooks.com

Printed in USA

10 9 8 7 6 5 4 3 2 1

First edition

Designs: Kristel Salgarollo
Artistic Direction: Joanna Perraudin
Illustrations and Technique Instructions: Céline Cantat
Photography: Pierre Nicou
(except for photos on pages 5, 9, 14, 15, 19, 23, 26, 29, 35, 38, 39, 40, 43, 47, 50, 53, 57, 66, 72, and 76, by Didier Barbecot)
Photo Styling: Marie-Paule Faure
Translation: Kathryn Fulton
Cover Design: Tessa Sweigert

Library of Congress Cataloging-in-Publication Data

Salgarollo, Kristel.
  Colorful crochet Afghans and pillows : 19 projects to brighten your home /
Kristel Salgarollo.
    pages cm
  ISBN 978-0-8117-1463-1
  1. Crocheting—Patterns. 2. Afghans (Coverlets) 3. Pillows. I. Title.
  TT825.S23 2014
  746.43'4—dc23
                    2014033769